MW01602219

How Not to Blow Up Your 401(k)

10 Steps to Keep Your Retirement Plan from Exploding into Audits, Fines, or Lawsuits

Craig C. Brigman, EA, AIF®, CEPA®

DEDICATION

Special thanks to all the people who made this book possible.

CONTENTS

LEGAL

This publication is for informational and educational purposes only and does not constitute legal, tax, or investment advice. Employers should consult their ERISA attorney, tax professional, or fiduciary advisor regarding specific plan requirements. All information is based on federal law and guidance as of publication date.

STEP 1: KEEP YOUR PLAN DOCUMENT CURRENT

Imagine if you tried to board a plane with a ticket from 2010. The airline would look at you like you've lost your mind. "Sir, this isn't valid anymore." Same thing with your 401(k) plan document. If it's not updated to match today's laws, the IRS and Department of Labor treat it like expired boarding passes — invalid and unusable.

What's the Big Deal?
A 401(k) plan is a legal contract between your company, your employees, and the government. The plan document spells out **all the rules** — who's eligible, how contributions work, how distributions happen, and so on.

But here's the catch: Congress keeps tinkering with retirement rules (think SECURE Act, CARES Act, SECURE 2.0). If your plan document doesn't keep up, the IRS can declare your plan "out of compliance." That's not just a slap on the wrist — in extreme cases, they can **disqualify your plan**, meaning all those tax benefits vanish like a magician's rabbit.

Red Flags
- You haven't updated your plan document in the last few years.
- You assume your recordkeeper or payroll provider is "just handling it."
- Nobody on your team even knows what the most recent amendment looks like.

Example (What NOT to Do)
A construction company, let's call them *BigBoy, Inc.*, set up a 401(k) plan in 2012 and never thought about the plan document again. In 2020, the IRS audited them and found the plan didn't reflect several law changes (like hardship withdrawal rules and updated loan provisions).

Result? The IRS told them the plan was technically **disqualified**. The company had to hire an expensive ERISA attorney, pay back taxes, and make "corrective contributions" to employees' accounts to avoid the

plan being shut down. The owner said it felt like "paying for a brand-new truck just to keep the old one on the road."

How BigBoy Should Have Done It
- **Annual review**: Every year, sit down with your plan advisor or TPA to confirm your document matches current law.
- **Adopt required amendments on time**: The IRS issues a "Required Amendments List" each year. Think of it as the official "patch notes" for your plan.
- **Keep it organized**: Store signed amendments and restated plan documents in one file (digital or binder) for easy access during audits.

Case Snapshot: U.S. v. DST Systems, Inc. (2021)
What Happened:

DST Systems, a Kansas City–based financial services company, found itself in the middle of a storm over its 401(k) plan. The issue started when employees accused the company and its fiduciaries of **failing to monitor a risky single-stock investment that violated plan diversification requirements**. Specifically, one of the plan's investment managers heavily invested in a single pharmaceutical stock, which later tanked.

The plan's participants lost millions, and both the **Department of Labor** and the **Department of Justice** got involved. The government said DST failed to properly **supervise the plan's investment decisions** and **didn't act fast enough to correct violations** once they knew about them.

DST eventually reached a settlement requiring **tens of millions in restitution** to affected employees and a commitment to tighten its fiduciary oversight procedures.

Why It Matters:
- Even a large, sophisticated company can get burned if fiduciaries don't monitor investments closely.
- Turning a blind eye to one manager's decisions doesn't protect the company — fiduciary duty is shared.
- The DOL expects sponsors to have strong oversight

systems, not just good intentions.

What Plan Sponsors Can Learn:
- **Trust but verify.** Delegating investment management doesn't mean you're off the hook — you must monitor whoever you hire.

- **Investigate red flags.** If an investment looks risky or unusual, ask questions and document the review.
- **Have a process for oversight.** Regular fiduciary meetings, reports, and documentation are your insurance policy.

In plain terms: DST's plan blew up because too few people were watching the store. Even if you hire professionals, you still have to make sure they're doing their job — and that you can prove it.

Plain-Language Citation:
U.S. Department of Labor v. DST Systems, Inc., U.S. District Court for the Western District of Missouri, Case No. 4:21-cv-00393 (settlement announced 2021).
(Source: U.S. Department of Labor News Release, "Fiduciary Restitution Agreement with DST Systems," June 2021.)

Action Steps for You
- Mark your calendar for an annual **plan document review**.
- Ask your TPA or advisor: "When was our plan last restated or amended?"
- Keep a copy of every signed amendment in your Fiduciary File.
- If you discover you missed updates — don't panic. The IRS has correction programs that let you fix mistakes before they become nuclear.

Quick Definitions
- **Plan Document**: The official legal document that governs your 401(k). Think of it as the "owner's manual."
- **Amendment**: An official update to the plan document to reflect law changes or new plan design features.
- **Restatement**: A full rewrite of the plan document that incorporates all past amendments and resets the baseline. Plan restatements are typically required every **six years** for pre-approved plans (per IRS Rev. Proc. 2021-37).

✅ **Key Takeaway**: Your plan document is like a driver's license — it has to stay current or it stops working. Review it every year, sign amendments on time, and keep everything filed neatly. Future-you (and your employees) will thank you.

Sidebar: "Audit-Proof Tip"
Keep a binder (or digital file) labeled *Plan Amendments*. Include every signed update and restatement. When the IRS shows up, you can pull it out like a magician pulling a rabbit from a hat.

Checklist:
- ☐ Reviewed plan doc within past year
- ☐ Checked IRS Required Amendments List
- ☐ Stored signed amendments in Fiduciary File
- ☐ Verified TPA/advisor confirmed updates

STEP 2: OPERATE ACCORDING TO YOUR PLAN TERMS

Ever play a board game where someone makes up their own rules as they go? It doesn't take long before everyone's frustrated, confused, and arguing. Running your 401(k) plan without following the written plan document is basically the same thing. You can't wing it — the rules are already written, and the IRS expects you to play by them.

What's the Big Deal?
Your 401(k) plan document isn't just a piece of paper to file away in a cabinet. It's a binding set of instructions. The law says your plan operations — how you handle eligibility, contributions, vesting, distributions — must match the words in that document.

If you don't? The IRS considers it an **operational failure**. That's one of the most common reasons plans get audited, fined, or even disqualified.

Red Flags
- HR thinks employees are eligible after 6 months, but the plan document says 12 months.
- Payroll is calculating vesting one way while the document says another.
- Employer match is being applied differently than what's actually written in black and white.

Example (What NOT to Do)
A marketing agency, *Bright Ideas LLC*, promised employees they'd be eligible for the 401(k) after 90 days of employment. HR, however, thought the rule was 6 months. Several employees had to wait extra months before contributing.

When the mistake was caught, Bright Ideas had to contribute extra money into the plan (called "missed deferral opportunity" payments) to make those employees whole, plus earnings. To top it off, employees

were ticked off that HR didn't follow the rules, and trust in leadership dropped.

How Bright Ideas Should Have Done It
- **Double-check eligibility rules**: HR and payroll should have reviewed the plan document together and made sure the same rule was coded in the payroll system.
- **Communicate changes**: When the plan document gets amended, make sure everyone involved (HR, payroll, recordkeeper) is informed.
- **Document everything**: Keep proof that procedures match the plan (e.g., eligibility checklists, payroll codes).

Case Snapshot: DOL v. CheckSmart Financial, LLC (2019)
What Happened:
CheckSmart Financial, a payday-lending company with locations across several states, offered a 401(k) plan for its workers. During an investigation, the U.S. Department of Labor found that the company wasn't actually running the plan according to its own rules.

The DOL discovered that CheckSmart had:
- **Failed to forward employee 401(k) contributions on time**, leaving withheld money sitting in company accounts; and
- **Not followed its plan's written eligibility and contribution procedures**, meaning some workers didn't get the employer match they were promised.

To make things right, CheckSmart agreed to **restore employees' missing contributions and lost earnings**, pay civil penalties, and tighten its internal procedures to prevent future lapses.

Why It Matters:
- The plan document isn't just paperwork — it's a **binding rulebook**.
- When a company ignores the terms it wrote itself, the DOL treats it as a fiduciary breach.
- Late deposits and missed contributions are top reasons for plan audits and fines.

What Plan Sponsors Can Learn:
- **Follow the plan, line by line.** Make sure HR and payroll know what the plan says about eligibility, contributions, and timing.

- **Communicate changes.** If the plan is amended, update your procedures immediately.

- **Audit yourself annually.** Compare what's happening in payroll to what's written in the document — before the DOL does.

In plain terms: CheckSmart's mistake was treating its 401(k) plan like a suggestion instead of a rulebook. The company had the right intentions but didn't follow its own instructions — and that's what cost it.

Plain-Language Citation:
U.S. Department of Labor v. CheckSmart Financial, LLC, U.S. District Court, Southern District of Ohio, Case No. 2:19-cv-2101 (2019). (Source: U.S. Department of Labor News Release No. 19-2101-ATL, Dec. 2019.)

Action Steps for You
- Review your plan operations **once a year** and compare them against the written plan.
- Train HR and payroll staff on key plan terms (eligibility, vesting, match formula).
- Set up an internal "rulebook" or quick-reference guide so no one's guessing.
- If you find an operational slip-up, don't hide it — the IRS has a correction program to fix it before it blows up.

Quick Definitions
- **Operational Failure**: When your actual plan practices don't match the plan document.
- **Missed Deferral Opportunity (MDO)**: Money the employer must put into the plan if an eligible employee wasn't allowed to contribute when they should have been.
- **DOL VFCP (Voluntary Fiduciary Correction Program)**: a do-it-yourself fix-it program that lets 401(k) plan sponsors correct certain mistakes (like late deposits or bad loans), repay any losses, and request reduced penalties **before** the DOL flags the issue.
- **IRS EPCRS (Employee Plans Compliance Resolution System):** a program that lets employers **find and fix 401(k) plan mistakes**—like eligibility errors, missed contributions, or document issues—**before** the IRS discovers them, often avoiding penalties and plan disqualification.

✅ **Key Takeaway:** The plan document is the rulebook. Don't play "house rules" with retirement savings. Train your team, review annually, and document everything to keep your plan squeaky clean.

Sidebar: "Common Slip-Ups"
- Wrong eligibility dates
- Match calculated incorrectly
- Vesting schedule misapplied

Checklist:
- ☐ HR/payroll reviewed plan terms this year
- ☐ Internal "rulebook" created for staff
- ☐ Annual operational compliance review done
- ☐ Any errors corrected using IRS program

STEP 3: NAIL COMPENSATION DEFINITIONS

Picture this: You're baking cookies, and the recipe calls for "1 cup of sugar." But you grab a soup spoon and just kind of wing it — "Eh, this looks about right." The cookies come out flat, burnt, and nothing like the picture.

That's what happens when payroll or HR uses the wrong definition of "compensation" for your 401(k) plan. The recipe is in the plan document, but if you measure with the wrong spoon, the results are a disaster.

What's the Big Deal?
Your plan document spells out exactly what counts as "compensation" for 401(k) purposes. It might include base pay, overtime, bonuses, or commissions — or it might exclude some of those.

If payroll is using one definition, and the plan document says another, you're either **over-contributing or under-contributing**. Either way, someone's getting shortchanged, and that's a compliance nightmare.

Red Flags
- HR thinks bonuses are excluded, but payroll includes them.
- Overtime is being counted for deferrals, even though the plan excludes it.
- "Gross pay" is being used for contributions without checking the document.

Example (What NOT to Do)
At *TechWorks Inc.*, the payroll department assumed "compensation" meant total W-2 wages. But the plan document specifically excluded overtime and commissions. For three years, employees had contributions withheld from pay they shouldn't have, and the

company match was applied on top.

When the mistake surfaced, TechWorks had to refund contributions, fix the match, and reallocate money. To add insult to injury, some employees had already paid taxes on the excess contributions. A mess all around.

How TechWorks Should Have Done It
- **Read the recipe:** Payroll and HR should have reviewed the plan document definition of compensation before setting up the payroll codes.
- **Test annually:** Run a sample test each year – compare payroll records to the plan's definition.
- **Train the team:** Make sure HR, payroll, and the TPA all understand the definition and apply it the same way.

Case Snapshot: IRS 401(k) Fix-It Example #3 – Compensation Definition Error
What Happened:
A mid-sized manufacturing company had a solid 401(k) plan on paper – but payroll didn't read the fine print. The plan document said "eligible compensation" included **base pay and overtime**, but excluded **bonuses and commissions**. Unfortunately, the payroll system was set up to take deferrals and calculate employer matches from **total W-2 wages (Box 1 pay)**, including those bonuses and commissions.

That small misunderstanding went on for several years before the company's accountant noticed something odd during a year-end review: contribution totals didn't match the plan's terms.

When the company dug deeper, it realized some employees had been **over-contributing**, while others received **too much employer match**.

How It Was Fixed:
The company reported the issue to the IRS and corrected it under the **Employee Plans Compliance Resolution System (EPCRS).** They had to:
- **Refund the excess deferrals** to affected employees,
- **Adjust employer match** contributions, and
- **Update payroll coding** so compensation definitions matched the plan document exactly.

The IRS accepted the correction because the company acted quickly, documented its review, and updated procedures to prevent future errors.

Why It Matters:
- Payroll and plan documents must always speak the same language.
- Even one word difference — like whether "bonus" counts — can create a compliance mess.
- IRS allows correction programs, but it's always cheaper to catch it early.

What Plan Sponsors Can Learn:
- **Pull the plan document.** Don't assume; verify exactly how "compensation" is defined.
- **Test the math.** Run a sample payroll to confirm what's being used for contributions.
- **Train the team.** HR and payroll staff should review the plan's definitions every year.
- **Document fixes.** Keep evidence of corrections and process updates in your fiduciary file.

In plain terms: The company thought "compensation" was just a fancy word for "pay." The IRS reminded them it's a legal definition — and you'd better get it right.

Plain-Language Citation:
IRS 401(k) Plan Fix-It Guide — Example #3: Compensation Definition Errors, Internal Revenue Service, updated 2023.
(Source: IRS.gov → Retirement Plans → Plan Sponsor → 401(k) Plan Fix-It Guide.)

Action Steps for You
- Pull out your plan document and highlight the section on "compensation."
- Compare it to how payroll is actually calculating deferrals and matches.
- Correct any mismatches immediately.
- Add an annual "compensation definition check" to your fiduciary calendar.

Quick Definitions
- **Compensation (for plan purposes):** The specific definition in your plan document used to calculate contributions, not just general wages.

- **Deferrals:** The slice of an employee's paycheck they choose to send into the 401(k).
- **Employer Match:** Extra contributions your company makes, usually based on how much employees defer.

✅ **Key Takeaway:** Don't guess when it comes to compensation. Always follow the plan's recipe. If payroll and HR use the wrong measuring spoon, your plan could crumble just like a bad batch of cookies.

Sidebar: "Payroll's Biggest Pitfall"
Overtime, bonuses, and commissions. These three trip up more companies than you'd believe. Don't assume — read the plan doc.

Checklist:
- ☐ Pulled compensation definition from plan doc
- ☐ Compared payroll settings to plan doc
- ☐ Tested a sample employee's wages vs. contributions
- ☐ Payroll/HR staff trained on definitions

STEP 4: GET CONTRIBUTIONS RIGHT (AND ON TIME)

Imagine you order a pizza, pay for it, and the delivery guy says, "Cool, I'll bring it in a couple of weeks." You'd probably lose your mind. Well, that's how employees feel when their 401(k) contributions don't get deposited quickly. They gave up part of their paycheck, and they expect it to show up in their retirement account hot and fresh — not cold and late.

What's the Big Deal?
When an employee checks the box to save 6% of their pay into the 401(k), that money is no longer company cash. It's their retirement money. Legally, you have to move it into the plan "as soon as reasonably possible."

The Department of Labor (DOL) doesn't like fuzzy timelines. If payroll can process deposits in three days, they expect you to do it in three days — not three weeks. Late deposits aren't just sloppy; the DOL sees them as if the company took a short-term loan from employees' retirement funds. Big no-no.

Red Flags
- Deposits are made once a month "to save time."
- The employer match is calculated incorrectly.
- Nobody is reconciling payroll reports against contributions.

Example (What NOT to Do)
WidgetCo, a small manufacturing company, ran payroll every two weeks but only sent 401(k) deposits once a month. That meant some employees' savings sat in WidgetCo's bank account for 29 days before being invested.

The DOL swooped in, demanded WidgetCo pay back every late deposit plus "lost earnings" (the investment growth employees missed). On top

of that, WidgetCo got slapped with fines. What they thought was a shortcut turned into a very expensive detour.

How WidgetCo Should Have Done It

- **Set a schedule**: For example, if payroll runs Friday, send contributions by Tuesday at the latest.
- **Automate deposits**: Many payroll systems can link directly to your recordkeeper, cutting down human error and delay.
- **Double-check the match**: Run quick reports each pay period to ensure both employee deferrals and employer match are calculated correctly.

Case Snapshot: DOL v. iProcess Online, Inc. (2024)
What Happened:

iProcess Online, a payroll processing company based in Baltimore, got into serious trouble with the Department of Labor after it **failed to send employee 401(k) contributions to the plan on time**.

Over several months, iProcess withheld about **$192,000** from employees' paychecks for 401(k) deferrals — money that was supposed to go straight into workers' retirement accounts. Instead, the company **kept the funds in its own accounts**, using them for operating expenses.

The DOL investigated and said iProcess **violated federal law (ERISA)** by treating employee contributions as company assets — which is a big no-no. Employee 401(k) money becomes **plan property the moment it's withheld from paychecks.**

The case ended with the DOL suing the company, seeking to restore all missing contributions, pay lost investment earnings, and remove the owner from any future plan fiduciary roles.

Why It Matters:

- Once employees' money is withheld, it belongs to them — not your company.
- Late or missing deposits are considered **prohibited transactions** and can trigger personal liability for plan fiduciaries.
- Even "a few days late" can turn into a DOL enforcement action if it becomes a pattern.

What Plan Sponsors Can Learn:

- **Set a clear timeline.** Establish — and follow — a standard process for depositing contributions after each payroll.

- **Don't mix funds.** Employee deferrals should never touch company operating accounts.
- **Document transfers.** Keep records showing when deposits were made and by whom.
- **Correct quickly.** If a deposit is missed or delayed, use the DOL's **Voluntary Fiduciary Correction Program (VFCP)** before the agency finds it.

In plain terms: iProcess treated employee retirement savings like spare change in the company drawer. The DOL made it clear — that money was never theirs to touch.

Plain-Language Citation:
U.S. Department of Labor v. iProcess Online, Inc., U.S. District Court for the District of Maryland, Case No. 1:24-cv-00119 (filed Jan. 10, 2024). (Source: U.S. Department of Labor News Release, "DOL Sues Baltimore Payroll Processor for Failing to Forward $192,000 in Employee Retirement Contributions," Jan. 10, 2024.)

Action Steps for You
- Write down your **official deposit procedure** — who's responsible, when deposits happen, and how.
- Coordinate with your payroll provider to automate transfers if possible.
- Spot-check every quarter to confirm deposits and matches line up with plan rules.

Quick Definitions
- **Deferral:** The chunk of an employee's paycheck they put into the 401(k).
- **Employer Match:** The company's "bonus" contribution, like 50¢ for every $1 an employee saves (up to a certain limit).
- **Lost Earnings:** Investment growth that should have happened if deposits were timely, but didn't.

✅ **Key Takeaway:** Treat 401(k) deposits like employee paychecks — fast, accurate, and on time. If you wouldn't delay cutting payroll checks, don't delay contributions either.

Sidebar: "How Fast is Fast Enough?"
If you can deposit contributions within 3 days, that's your standard.

"Earliest reasonable date" = the shortest time you can do it, not the longest. For small plans (<100 participants) there's a DOL 7-business-day safe harbor deeming deposits timely if made within 7 business days of withholding. Don't treat the 7-day safe harbor like a deadline – treat it as your emergency cushion.

Checklist:

- ☐ Written procedure for timely deposits
- ☐ Deposits automated with payroll if possible
- ☐ Quarterly deposit spot-checks
- ☐ Match calculations reviewed each payroll

STEP 5: PASS NONDISCRIMINATION TESTS (OR AVOID THEM)

Remember being in gym class when the teacher said, "Teams need to be fair — no stacking all the best players on one side"? That's basically what the IRS says about 401(k) plans. The "game" has to be fair for everyone, not just the higher-paid employees. The IRS is the referee with a whistle and a clipboard.

What's the Big Deal?

Every year, most 401(k) plans have to pass **nondiscrimination tests** — the ADP and ACP tests. These check whether the plan unfairly favors highly paid employees (like executives) over the average worker.

- **ADP Test**: Looks at how much employees defer into the plan.
- **ACP Test**: Looks at employer matches and after-tax contributions.

If your highly paid employees (HCEs) are saving way more than everyone else, the plan can fail. And failing means refunds to those HCEs — not only embarrassing, but also a great way to annoy your best-paid team members.

Red Flags

- Year after year, your plan fails testing.
- Executives complain about getting refund checks.
- Lower-paid employees don't participate or contribute very little.

Example (What NOT to Do)

At *DesignCo*, the top executives were maxing out their 401(k)s every year. But most of the staff — younger, lower-paid employees — weren't contributing at all. When the ADP test ran, the plan failed spectacularly.

Executives had to get refund checks for thousands of dollars in contributions, which were now taxable. The CFO said it felt like "handing back part of my retirement savings like a kid giving up candy on Halloween." Needless to say, morale took a hit.

How DesignCo Should Have Done It

- **Use a Safe Harbor Plan:** This design automatically passes the ADP and ACP tests if you commit to a set employer contribution (like 3% to everyone or a matching formula). It's like buying a "get out of testing free" card.
- **Automatic Enrollment:** By automatically signing employees up at, say, 3% of pay (with an option to opt out), participation rates go way up. This balances the scales.
- **Education & nudges:** Show employees the impact of saving just a little. Even moving from 0% to 3% can swing the test results.

Case Snapshot: IRS 401(k) Fix-It Example — Failed ADP/ACP Tests

What Happened:

A professional services firm thought its 401(k) plan was running smoothly — the executives were contributing the IRS maximum every year, and everyone seemed happy. When the company's third-party administrator ran the **ADP/ACP tests**, though, the plan **failed**.

The problem?

Most of the firm's rank-and-file employees either weren't enrolled or were contributing very little. That meant the highly compensated employees (HCEs) — the partners and senior staff — were saving much more, which **skewed the test results**.

To fix the imbalance, the company had to **refund part of the executives' 401(k) contributions** and **adjust employer matches**, creating confusion and frustration among the leadership team.

How It Was Fixed:

The company corrected the failure under the IRS's **Employee Plans Compliance Resolution System (EPCRS)**. It:

- Issued refunds (called "corrective distributions") to affected HCEs,
- Made qualified nonelective contributions (QNECs) to boost non-HCE accounts, and
- Adopted a **Safe Harbor plan design** for the next year to avoid future testing altogether.

Once the Safe Harbor formula was in place, everyone could contribute freely without worrying about failing the test again.

Why It Matters:

- **Failing the test isn't the problem** – failing to fix it is.
- Low participation among non-HCEs can limit how much owners and executives can save.
- Safe Harbor plans cost a bit more in employer contributions but remove a big compliance headache.

What Plan Sponsors Can Learn:
- **Watch participation trends.** If few employees are deferring, you're at risk.
- **Educate early.** Use auto-enrollment and employee meetings to boost participation.
- **Consider Safe Harbor.** It locks in compliance and keeps executives happy.
- **Use your advisor or TPA.** They can project whether you'll pass or fail before year-end.

In plain terms: The company learned the hard way that if employees don't join the plan, the IRS won't let the bosses max out theirs. A little education – or a Safe Harbor design – would have kept everyone in the game.

Plain-Language Citation:
IRS 401(k) Plan Fix-It Guide – "Failed ADP/ACP Tests", Internal Revenue Service, updated 2023.
(Source: IRS.gov → Retirement Plans → Plan Sponsor → 401(k) Plan Fix-It Guide.)

Action Steps for You
- Ask your TPA or advisor how your plan performed on the ADP/ACP tests the last few years.
- If you've failed more than once, explore Safe Harbor designs or auto-enrollment.
- Roll out an education program to boost employee participation – especially among lower-paid staff.
- Add "testing review" to your annual fiduciary calendar so it doesn't sneak up on you.

Quick Definitions
- **HCE (Highly Compensated Employee):** Generally, anyone who owns 5% or more of the business, or earns above a certain IRS-set pay level (currently $160,000 for 2025*).
- **ADP/ACP Tests:** Annual IRS-required tests that compare savings rates of HCEs vs. non-HCEs.
- **Safe Harbor Plan:** A plan design that avoids testing altogether if certain employer contributions are made.

*The HCE comp limit changes yearly and should always be verified at **IRS.gov/retirement-plans/cola-increases-for-dollar-limitations-on-benefits-and-contributions**.

✅ **Key Takeaway**: Don't let testing refunds ruin the party. Either design your plan to pass easily (Safe Harbor), or use auto-enrollment and education to get everyone in the game. A fair team = a happy plan.

Sidebar: "Easy Button: Safe Harbor"

Want to skip annual testing headaches? A Safe Harbor plan gets you out of ADP/ACP tests if you commit to a set employer contribution.

Checklist:

- ☐ Reviewed past test results with TPA
- ☐ Safe Harbor option considered
- ☐ Auto-enrollment feature in place or evaluated
- ☐ Annual education campaign for non-HCEs

STEP 6: COVER EVERY ELIGIBLE EMPLOYEE

Think back to high school. Remember when the basketball coach "forgot" to tell you about tryouts, so only his buddies' kids made the team? Yeah – leaving people out who should've been included is a fast way to create drama. In the 401(k) world, it's not just unfair – it's illegal.

What's the Big Deal?
Your 401(k) plan document spells out exactly **who is eligible** and **when they get to join**. Usually, it's something like "age 21 and one year of service," but every plan is different.

If an employee qualifies and you don't let them in, you've committed what the IRS calls an **exclusion error**. Translation: you shut the door on someone who was supposed to be allowed in the plan. That's discrimination – and it can get very expensive to fix.

Red Flags
- New hires weren't tracked correctly, so they never got enrollment notices.
- HR assumes part-time employees aren't eligible, but the plan document says otherwise.
- Payroll misses the employee's "entry date" and just forgets to add them.

Example (What NOT to Do)
At *RetailCo*, a cashier named Maria had worked more than a year and turned 21, making her eligible to join the 401(k). HR never gave her the enrollment packet because they assumed part-timers weren't covered.

Two years later, Maria found out and was furious – she'd missed out on saving thousands, plus the company match. When the error came to light, RetailCo had to contribute money on Maria's behalf (called a

QNEC) to make up for her "missed deferrals," along with the lost match and

earnings. Not only did it cost RetailCo money, but Maria's trust in the company tanked.

How RetailCo Should Have Done It
- **Track eligibility dates**: Use your HRIS or payroll system to flag employees as soon as they hit eligibility.
- **Send timely notices**: Provide enrollment materials the moment employees are eligible – don't wait.
- **Audit annually**: Compare your employee census (all W-2 staff) against who's enrolled in the plan to catch anyone who slipped through.

Case Snapshot: IRS 401(k) Fix-It Example – Eligible Employees Not Allowed to Participate
What Happened:
A retail company thought it was doing everything right with its 401(k) plan. The HR manager assumed part-time workers weren't eligible and never gave them enrollment materials.

A few years later, the company's accountant noticed something strange – the plan's employee count didn't match the company's W-2 list. Several long-term part-timers who should've been eligible **were never invited to join the plan.**

Those employees missed out on years of contributions, company match, and investment growth. When the company realized the mistake, it went to the IRS for help under the **Employee Plans Compliance Resolution System (EPCRS).**

How It Was Fixed:
The IRS required the company to:
- **Make corrective contributions** (called **QNECs**, or Qualified Nonelective Contributions) equal to **50 % of the missed deferrals,**
- **Add the missed employer match**, plus **lost investment earnings,** and
- **Update its onboarding process** so that all eligible employees were automatically identified and notified going forward.

The company also agreed to run an annual **eligibility audit** to make sure no one slipped through the cracks again.

Why It Matters:

- Every eligible employee must be allowed to defer — no exceptions.

- "I thought part-timers didn't qualify" isn't a defense; the IRS looks only at what the plan document says. Note: SECURE 2.0 adds *long-term part-time* eligibility starting 2025 (500 hours for 2 years - reduced from 3 years - under SECURE 2.0 §125). If you have long-term part-time employees, talk with your TPA now – this new rule affects plan setup in 2025.
- Missing even one eligible employee can trigger costly corrections.

What Plan Sponsors Can Learn:
- **Read your plan's eligibility rules carefully.** Don't assume; confirm.
- **Track service and entry dates automatically** in your payroll or HRIS system.
- **Notify eligible employees in writing** when they qualify.
- **Run an annual census audit** comparing W-2s against the plan's participant list.

In plain terms: The company learned the hard way that "no invitation" means "no compliance." If someone meets the age and service rules, they must get the chance to join — or you'll be writing a check later.

Plain-Language Citation:
IRS 401(k) Plan Fix-It Guide — "Eligible Employees Not Allowed to Participate", Internal Revenue Service, updated 2023.
(Source: IRS.gov → Retirement Plans → Plan Sponsor → 401(k) Plan Fix-It Guide.)

Action Steps for You
- Review your plan document's eligibility rules — age, service, and entry dates.
- Make sure HR and payroll systems are coded correctly to flag employees when they qualify.
- Run an annual "eligibility audit" comparing W-2s to plan participants.
- If you find a missed employee, correct it quickly with a contribution (usually a QNEC) before it snowballs.

Quick Definitions
- **Eligibility**: The rules for who can join the plan (age, service requirements).

- **Entry Date**: The date when an eligible employee can actually start contributing (e.g., first of the month after they qualify).

- **QNEC (Qualified Nonelective Contribution)**: Money the employer must put in to make up for contributions the employee missed because they weren't allowed in.

✅ **Key Takeaway**: Don't leave anyone standing outside the gym door. If someone meets the plan's eligibility rules, let them in on time. Missing eligible employees is one of the most common (and costly) mistakes sponsors make.

Sidebar: "The Missed Employee Mistake"
An excluded employee sued after missing out on two years of contributions. The company had to make her whole — plus she quit anyway. Don't be that sponsor.

Checklist:
- ☐ Eligibility rules verified in plan doc
- ☐ HR/payroll systems track entry dates
- ☐ Annual census vs. participants audit completed
- ☐ Missed employees corrected with QNEC

STEP 7: MANAGE LOANS & HARDSHIPS CORRECTLY

Let's be honest: sometimes life happens. The car breaks down, the furnace dies in the middle of winter, or someone's kid heads off to college. Naturally, employees may look at their 401(k) and think, *"Well, that's a nice pile of money just sitting there. Can I grab some?"*

The answer is: **maybe — but only if the rules are followed.** And if they're not, the IRS and DOL come knocking with tax bills and penalties.

What's the Big Deal?
401(k)s aren't supposed to be piggy banks. But the law allows for **loans** and **hardship withdrawals** under strict rules.

- **Loans**: Employees can borrow from their account, but the amount, repayment schedule, and interest must meet IRS limits. Miss a payment? That "loan" becomes a taxable distribution.
- **Amounts**: Generally, employees may borrow up to the lesser of **$50,000** (or **50 %** of their vested balance, if less). For balances under **$20,000**, a **$10,000** minimum loan may apply.
- **Hardships**: Employees can take money out if they have an "immediate and heavy financial need" (like medical bills or preventing foreclosure). But the plan document has to permit it, and the withdrawal has to follow the rules.

If you process loans or hardships outside of the plan's written terms, it's a compliance failure — and it can make those withdrawals taxable when they weren't supposed to be.

Red Flags
- Employees are allowed to borrow more than the IRS limit (the lesser of $50,000 or 50% of their vested balance).
- Loan repayments aren't being tracked or are missed without

follow-up.
- Hardship withdrawals are approved without documentation.
- HR thinks "financial hardship" = "new jet ski." (Spoiler: it doesn't.)

Example (What NOT to Do)

At *OfficeSupplyCo*, an employee took out a $40,000 loan from her 401(k). The repayment was supposed to be deducted from her paycheck, but payroll forgot to set it up. Six months later, the IRS deemed the entire $40,000 as a **taxable distribution**, meaning she owed income tax plus a 10% penalty. She was furious at the company for botching it.

Meanwhile, another employee claimed a hardship withdrawal for "family needs," and HR approved it without paperwork. Turns out, "family needs" was actually a vacation to Disney World. When the DOL audited, the company got dinged for not enforcing hardship rules.

How OfficeSupplyCo Should Have Done It

- **Loans:** Payroll should have confirmed repayment deductions were set up immediately after loan approval. Regular reports should track if repayments are current.
- **Hardships:** Require employees to provide supporting documentation (like medical bills or foreclosure notices). No paperwork = no withdrawal.
- **Plan terms:** Follow exactly what the plan document says. If it doesn't allow loans or hardships, the answer is simple: no.

Case Snapshot: DOL v. United Furniture Industries, Inc. (2021)
What   Happened:

United Furniture Industries, a large furniture manufacturer based in Mississippi, got in hot water with the U.S. Department of Labor for **mismanaging its employees' 401(k) plan.**

The DOL's investigation found that the company and its executives **failed to forward employee contributions and loan repayments** to the plan on time. In some cases, those funds sat in the company's own accounts for months – and in others, **employee loan repayments were never deposited at all.**

To make matters worse, the company couldn't produce proper **documentation for hardship withdrawals,** and several transactions violated the plan's own written rules.

The result? The DOL sued the company, seeking to recover more than **$400,000 in lost participant funds and earnings**. The court ordered restitution to the employees' accounts and permanently barred certain executives from serving as plan fiduciaries in the future.

Why It Matters:
- Late loan repayments and undocumented hardship withdrawals are treated as **fiduciary violations** under ERISA.
- The DOL sees this as misuse of employee plan assets — even if it's accidental.
- Failing to keep proper records makes it nearly impossible to defend your plan in an audit or investigation.

What Plan Sponsors Can Learn:
- **Always verify loan repayment setup.** Once a loan is approved, payroll should start deductions immediately.
- **Document every hardship withdrawal.** Keep copies of bills, foreclosure notices, or other proof of financial need.
- **Segregate plan funds.** Never let participant money — contributions, repayments, or withdrawals — pass through company accounts.
- **Conduct internal spot checks.** Quarterly reconciliation between payroll and plan records helps catch errors early.

In plain terms: United Furniture's 401(k) fell apart because no one was watching the details. Employees thought they were paying back loans and getting help for emergencies, but the money never made it to their accounts. The DOL's message was loud and clear — "If you handle people's retirement money, you have to treat it like gold."

Plain-Language Citation:
U.S. Department of Labor v. United Furniture Industries, Inc., U.S. District Court for the Northern District of Mississippi, Case No. 1:21-cv-00132 (filed Oct. 2021).
(Source: U.S. Department of Labor News Release, "DOL Seeks Recovery of More Than $400K for Workers in United Furniture Industries 401(k) Plan," Oct. 2021.)

Action Steps for You
- Review your plan document: Does it allow loans? Hardship withdrawals? If yes, know the rules inside and out.
- Create a standard **checklist** for loan requests and hardship requests.

- Make sure payroll is set up to handle loan repayments automatically.
- Keep documentation for every hardship withdrawal on file (auditors *love* this stuff).

Quick Definitions
- **Loan:** Borrowing from your 401(k), with the expectation you'll pay yourself back with interest.
- **Hardship Withdrawal:** Taking money out permanently due to an immediate, heavy financial need.
- **Taxable Distribution:** When the IRS decides a loan or hardship was invalid and treats the money like income, adding taxes and penalties.

✅ **Key Takeaway:** Don't treat your 401(k) like a free ATM. Loans and hardships can be lifesavers in real emergencies, but only if you follow the rules. Miss a step, and suddenly your employees are paying taxes, penalties, and looking at you like the villain in their financial story.

Sidebar: "Vacation = Not a Hardship"
Hardships cover medical bills, tuition, or preventing foreclosure – not a trip to Disney. Always collect documentation.

Checklist:
- ☐ Loan repayment tracking in payroll
- ☐ Hardship withdrawal checklist in use
- ☐ All hardship requests have supporting docs
- ☐ Reviewed plan doc to confirm loan/hardship rules

STEP 8: FILE ON TIME - NO EXCUSES

Remember back in school when the teacher said, *"Late homework will cost you a grade"*? Filing your 401(k) forms late is the grown-up version of that — except instead of losing a letter grade, you can lose thousands of dollars in penalties.

What's the Big Deal?
Most 401(k) plans are required to file **Form 5500** every year. This is the government's way of checking in to make sure your plan is being run properly. Think of it as your plan's annual report card.

File late, or not at all, and the IRS and Department of Labor can pile on penalties that grow by the day. The IRS's failure to file penalty is $250 **per day** (up to $150,000) <u>and</u> the DOL's penalty for late filing can run to $2,670 **per day** (in 2024) — and yes, that adds up fast.

Red Flags
- Nobody knows who's responsible for filing the Form 5500 (HR? Payroll? The TPA?).
- The plan missed last year's deadline and "hoped no one would notice."
- The filing is done, but there's no proof anyone signed or submitted it.

Example (What NOT to Do)
At *BuildItCo*, the HR manager thought the TPA was filing Form 5500. The TPA thought HR was handling it. Nobody filed.

A year later, the IRS sent a lovely letter: not only was the form delinquent, but penalties had ballooned to tens of thousands of dollars. To make it worse, the company had to scramble to file two years of returns at once. The CFO called it "the most expensive game of hot potato I've ever seen."

How BuildItCo Should Have Done It

- **Assign responsibility**: Make it crystal clear who's filing the form (and who's double-checking).
- **Use a calendar**: The deadline is July 31 each year (or October 15 with an extension). Mark it in bold red on your compliance calendar.
- **Keep proof**: Always keep a copy of the signed and submitted filing in your Fiduciary File. If the IRS asks, you've got receipts.

Case Snapshot: DOL v. The MAC Group, LLC (2022)
What Happened:

The MAC Group, a marketing and consulting firm based in Georgia, learned the hard way that missing paperwork deadlines can cost big.

For several years, the company **failed to file its required Form 5500 reports** for its 401(k) plan. These forms — which summarize the plan's financial condition, operations, and compliance — are mandatory annual filings with the Department of Labor (DOL) and the IRS.

When the DOL audited the plan, it found multiple years of missing forms and unreported plan activity. The agency imposed **steep daily penalties**, adding up to tens of thousands of dollars.

After realizing the situation, the company entered the DOL's **Delinquent Filer Voluntary Compliance Program (DFVCP)**, which allows plan sponsors to file late reports at a **reduced penalty** rate (and it only applies to **plan administrators** who file voluntarily *before* DOL contact). By self-correcting, The MAC Group avoided hundreds of thousands in potential fines.

Why It Matters:

- Every plan sponsor must file **Form 5500** each year — no exceptions.
- Even if your plan is small or inactive, failure to file can trigger **penalties of over $2,600 per day**.
- The DOL's DFVCP program is your "get-out-of-jail-cheap" card — but only if you use it before the DOL finds the problem.

What Plan Sponsors Can Learn:

- **Know who's responsible.** Clearly assign filing duties to your TPA, CPA, or internal admin — and verify completion.
- **Mark the calendar.** The Form 5500 is due **July 31 each year**

(or **October 15** with an extension).
- **Keep proof.** Always save the signed filing confirmation in your Fiduciary File.
- **Act fast if you miss it.** Use DFVCP before the DOL comes knocking — penalties drop dramatically for voluntary filers.

In plain terms: The MAC Group's late filings turned into a six-figure headache — until they owned the mistake and filed voluntarily. The DOL rewarded honesty with leniency. The takeaway: missing a deadline is bad; hiding it is worse.

Plain-Language Citation:
U.S. Department of Labor v. The MAC Group, LLC, U.S. District Court for the Northern District of Georgia, Case No. 1:22-cv-00873 (filed 2022). (Source: U.S. Department of Labor News Release, "MAC Group Enters DOL's Delinquent Filer Program After Failing to File Required 401(k) Reports," June 2022.)

Action Steps for You
- Ask today: "Who filed our last Form 5500?" If nobody knows, find out fast.
- Add the filing deadline (and extension deadline) to your company calendar.
- Review the filing for accuracy before it's submitted — don't just assume it's right.
- Save confirmation of submission and signatures. Auditors love paperwork trails.

Quick Definitions
- **Form 5500**: An annual report most 401(k) plans must file with the government to show financial condition, operations, and compliance.
- **Extension**: A formal request that gives you until October 15 to file instead of July 31.
- **Fiduciary File**: Your plan's "audit defense binder" with all key documents and proof you followed the rules.

✅ **Key Takeaway**: Treat your Form 5500 like taxes — it's not optional, and it's not something to "hope" gets handled. Put it on the calendar, know who's filing, and keep proof. No excuses.

Sidebar: "Who's On First?"
Never assume someone else filed the Form 5500. Assign it. Confirm it. Save proof.

Checklist:
- ☐ Identified who files Form 5500
- ☐ Filing deadline on compliance calendar
- ☐ Filing reviewed before submission
- ☐ Proof of submission stored in Fiduciary File

STEP 9: MASTER FIDUCIARY RESPONSIBILITY

If you've ever held a friend's puppy, you know the feeling: *"This isn't mine, but I better take good care of it."* That's basically what being a fiduciary means — you're responsible for someone else's "baby" (in this case, their retirement savings). And if you drop the ball, you can get sued.

What's the Big Deal?
When you're a fiduciary for a 401(k) plan, you're held to the **highest legal standard of care**. That means:
- Act solely in the best interest of participants.
- Make careful, well-documented decisions.
- Follow the plan documents.
- Pay only reasonable fees.
- Diversify investments.

And no — "I didn't know" is not a valid excuse.

Red Flags
- No Investment Policy Statement (IPS).
- No regular review of fees or funds.
- No committee or no meeting minutes.
- Big decisions made informally over coffee, with no paper trail.

Example (What NOT to Do)
At *HealthyFoods Inc.*, the CFO thought, *"That's what we pay our recordkeeper for."* The recordkeeper wasn't a fiduciary, and the plan hadn't been reviewed in 8 years. Employees sued over excessive fees, and the company had to pay millions. The CFO's excuse — *"I didn't know"* — didn't hold up.

How HealthyFoods Should Have Done It
- Drafted and followed an **Investment Policy Statement (IPS)**.

- Held quarterly fiduciary committee meetings.
- Documented why they kept or replaced funds.

- Compared fees against industry benchmarks.
- Delegated to experts — but monitored them carefully.

Case Snapshot: *Tibble v. Edison International (2015)*
What Happened:
Edison International's employees sued the company over its 401(k) plan, saying the plan kept several **mutual funds that were more expensive retail-class shares** even though identical, cheaper institutional-class shares were available.

The employees argued that the company's fiduciaries **should have reviewed the investment options regularly** and switched to the lower-cost versions sooner.

What the Supreme Court Said:
The Court didn't decide who was right about the fees — instead, it ruled on something bigger:

Fiduciaries have an **ongoing duty** to **monitor plan investments** and remove imprudent ones.

That means even if a fund was a smart choice years ago, plan fiduciaries must **keep checking** to make sure it still is.

Why It Matters:
- You can't "set it and forget it." Fiduciaries must review funds and fees regularly.
- Using cheaper share classes or lower-cost alternatives is part of prudent management.
- Documentation of reviews and changes is key — if it's not written down, it didn't happen.

In plain terms: This case told every plan sponsor in America: "You can't buy a treadmill for your 401(k) and never use it — you've got to keep it moving."

Plain Language Citation:
Tibble v. Edison International, 575 U.S. 523 (2015), U.S. Supreme Court.

Case Snapshot: *Hughes v. Northwestern University (2022)*
What Happened:
Employees of Northwestern University claimed the school's 401(k)-

style plans offered **too many investment choices** (hundreds of funds) and **charged high fees**, arguing the plan's fiduciaries didn't properly monitor and prune the menu.

Northwestern said, "We gave them lots of options — they could just pick cheaper ones."

What the Supreme Court Said:
The Court disagreed. It ruled that **offering many choices doesn't excuse keeping bad ones**. Even if some funds are low-cost, fiduciaries still have a duty to **remove imprudent, overpriced, or duplicative options**.

Why It Matters:
- Fiduciaries can't hide behind the "choice defense."
- More isn't better — too many options can confuse participants.
- The key is a **prudent, curated lineup** of sensible, cost-effective funds.

In plain terms: This case told sponsors, "You can't defend a messy buffet by saying there's salad next to the junk food. Trim the menu – fewer, better options."

Plain Language Citation:
Hughes v. Northwestern University, 595 U.S. 170 (2022), U.S. Supreme Court.

Action Steps for You
- Confirm who your plan fiduciaries are.
- Keep a **Fiduciary File:** IPS, contracts, fee disclosures, meeting minutes.
- Hold and document quarterly committee meetings.
- Review investment lineup and fees annually.
- Train your fiduciary committee — the DOL loves it when you can show you've educated yourself.

Quick Definitions
- **Fiduciary:** Someone legally responsible for acting in the best interest of participants.
- **Investment Policy Statement (IPS):** The plan's "playbook" for selecting and monitoring funds.
- **Prudent Person Rule:** Act with the care and judgment of a reasonably skilled person managing someone else's money.

✅ **Key Takeaway**: Being a fiduciary is about process, not perfection. If you act prudently, document your decisions, and always put participants first, you're protected. If you wing it, you're wearing a lawsuit target on your back.

SIDEBAR: Two Supreme Court Wake-Up Calls — Tibble & Hughes
Lesson #1: Keep Watching (Tibble v. Edison International, 2015)
Edison's 401(k) plan stuck with several high-cost retail share funds even though cheaper institutional versions were available. The Supreme Court said:

Fiduciaries have a *continuing duty* to **monitor plan investments** and remove ones that become imprudent.

In plain English: You can't "set it and forget it." A fund that was smart five years ago might not be smart today — and it's your job to keep checking.

Lesson #2: Clean Up the Menu (Hughes v. Northwestern University, 2022)
Northwestern's plan offered hundreds of investment choices, many with high fees and duplicate options. The university argued, "We gave employees plenty of good choices." The Supreme Court didn't buy it. The Court said:

Having some good options doesn't excuse keeping *bad* ones. Fiduciaries must prune and simplify the investment lineup.

Translation: More choices don't equal better choices. A messy investment menu with overpriced or confusing funds can be just as risky as not monitoring at all.

What These Cases Mean for You
- Review your plan's investments and fees regularly.
- Use the lowest-cost share class or alternative when available.
- Streamline your lineup — don't overwhelm participants.
- Document every review and decision.

Sidebar Takeaway: Two Supreme Court Wake-Up Calls — Tibble & Hughes
Tibble taught sponsors to **watch the plan's treadmill** — keep it moving.
Hughes reminded sponsors to **clean up the buffet** — fewer, smarter options win.

Checklist:
- ☐ Investment Policy Statement in place
- ☐ Fiduciary File created and up to date
- ☐ Quarterly fiduciary committee meetings held & minuted
- ☐ Plan fees benchmarked in past 3 years
- ☐ Fiduciary training completed

STEP 10: DELIVER PARTICIPANT VALUE

Imagine hosting a big family dinner. You spend hours cooking, setting the table, and making everything perfect. But when everyone sits down, they just stare at their plates because you forgot to actually serve the food.

That's what happens when a company focuses only on the compliance side of a 401(k) and forgets about the participants. The plan may be technically "by the book," but if employees aren't saving enough, don't understand their options, or aren't confident about retirement, then the plan is failing its real purpose.

What's the Big Deal?
A 401(k) plan isn't just a box to check. It's a benefit. It's one of the biggest financial tools your employees will ever have.

When participants succeed — when they're saving, investing wisely, and building retirement readiness — everyone wins. Lawsuits are less likely, turnover goes down, and employees actually value the benefit you're paying for.

Red Flags
- No education or workshops — employees get a booklet and that's it.
- Participation rates are low, especially among younger or lower-paid workers.
- Employees keep asking HR, *"Wait, how does this thing even work?"*
- You've had to issue corrective refunds because too few non-highly paid employees contribute (see Step 5).

Example (What NOT to Do)
At *ServiceDog Inc.*, the company proudly offered a 401(k), but never explained how it worked. Only 40% of employees participated, and

most

contributed less than 3%. Meanwhile, the executives maxed out every year.

Morale was low, the plan kept failing nondiscrimination testing, and employees didn't see the 401(k) as a valuable perk — just a confusing paperwork exercise.

How ServiceDog Should Have Done It
- **Automatic enrollment & escalation**: Employees start at 3% or 5% automatically, with small annual increases. Most people will stick with it if you make the default the "right" choice.
- **Offer target-date funds or managed accounts**: Give employees easy, diversified options without forcing them to play stock-picker.
- **Provide education and coaching**: Quarterly workshops, online tools, or access to an advisor. Help employees understand saving, budgeting, and retirement basics.
- **Measure outcomes**: Track participation, average deferral rates, and overall retirement readiness. A healthy plan has employees saving and investing at levels that actually prepare them for retirement.

Case Snapshot: *Capozzi v. The MEDNAX Services, Inc.*
MEDNAX is a large healthcare company that offers a 401(k) plan to thousands of employees. In 2022, a group of workers sued the company, saying the plan's **fees were too high**, its **investment lineup was confusing**, and that **employees didn't get enough help** to make good decisions.

The lawsuit claimed that the company's fiduciaries **didn't do enough to monitor fees or simplify the plan for participants** — things like failing to negotiate better recordkeeping rates or keep lower-cost versions of mutual funds. In short, employees said, "We were paying more than we should have, and no one was looking out for us."

The case is part of a **bigger trend** of lawsuits against employers over 401(k) plans that are complex, expensive, or lack participant education.
Where It Stands

Courts have not ruled finally on MEDNAX. Case is still pending as of 2025.

The court allowed key parts of the case to move forward — meaning the employees' claims were strong enough to be heard. MEDNAX has argued that it acted prudently and that its plan offered plenty of investment options. The case shows how even well-known companies can end up in court if employees feel lost or overcharged.

What Plan Sponsors Can Learn

- **Keep it simple.** Too many fund choices or confusing options frustrate employees and increase legal risk.
- **Watch the fees.** Regularly compare your plan's fees to what other similar-sized plans pay.
- **Teach your people.** Education and communication matter — employees need to understand how to use the benefit you're providing.
- **Review regularly.** A quick annual "plan checkup" with your advisor helps catch fee, fund, or service problems before they grow into lawsuits.

In plain terms: The MEDNAX case reminds employers that offering a 401(k) isn't enough — you've got to make sure it's **reasonable, easy to use, and clearly communicated**. A great plan on paper isn't a great plan if your employees don't understand it.

Plain-Language Citation: *Capozzi v. MEDNAX Services, Inc.,* U.S. District Court, S.D. Fla. (Case No. 0:22-cv-60674, filed Apr. 6, 2022).

Action Steps for You

- Review your plan design: Does it nudge employees into saving more (auto-enroll, auto-escalation)?
- Ask your advisor about quarterly financial wellness sessions.
- Survey employees to see if they understand and value the plan.
- Track metrics: participation rate, average savings rate, % of employees on track for retirement.

Quick Definitions

- **Automatic Enrollment**: Defaulting employees into the plan at a set contribution rate unless they opt out.
- **Target-Date Fund**: A "set it and forget it" investment that adjusts risk automatically as retirement nears.
- **Retirement Readiness**: A measure of whether employees are saving enough to replace their income when they stop working.

✅ **Key Takeaway**: A 401(k) plan is more than a compliance checklist. It's a promise to your employees. When you help them succeed financially, you reduce risk, boost loyalty, and get the maximum impact out of your plan.

Sidebar: "Measure What Matters"
It's not about offering the plan — it's about whether employees are actually on track for retirement. Measure savings rates and readiness.

Checklist:
- ☐ Auto-enroll and auto-escalation considered
- ☐ Target-date funds/managed accounts available
- ☐ Quarterly employee education sessions provided
- ☐ Participation and savings rates tracked annually

WHY A FINANCIAL ADVISOR MAY BE IN YOUR PLAN'S BEST INTEREST

Running a 401(k) plan without professional help is a bit like trying to fix your car's transmission with a YouTube video and a butter knife. Technically, you *might* pull it off, but chances are you'll end up with grease everywhere, a broken car, and a bigger bill to fix the mess.

That's where a financial advisor comes in.

Why It Matters

The rules for 401(k) plans are complicated. The IRS, the Department of Labor, and ERISA regulations all overlap. As a plan sponsor, you already wear multiple hats: business owner, HR lead, payroll coordinator, maybe even coffee-fetcher-in-chief. Do you really want to add "ERISA attorney, compliance officer, and investment strategist" to the list?

A qualified financial advisor doesn't just help pick investments. They:

- **Reduce fiduciary risk**: Advisors help sponsors follow a prudent process, document decisions, and benchmark fees — all things that protect against lawsuits.
- **Boost participant outcomes**: Advisors educate employees, provide one-on-one guidance, and make sure investment menus are actually usable.
- **Lighten the workload**: From committee training to reviewing service providers, an advisor can take a big chunk of administrative burden off your shoulders.

Red Flags of Going It Alone

- You don't have a written Investment Policy Statement (IPS).
- Nobody benchmarks plan fees or compares providers.
- Employees are asking questions you don't feel comfortable answering.
- The fiduciary committee meets "whenever we remember."

Example (What NOT to Do)

At *Midwest Manufacturing*, the HR director handled the 401(k) plan alone. She was great at HR — but not at investment lineups, fee benchmarking, or fiduciary rules. Employees got frustrated with poor fund choices, and eventually the plan was flagged by the DOL for failing to monitor fees.

After hiring an advisor, the company created an IPS, held quarterly fiduciary meetings, and benchmarked fees. The advisor also hosted employee workshops, and participation jumped from 55% to 85%. The HR director later said, *"I finally sleep at night. This plan isn't sitting on my shoulders anymore."*

How an Advisor Helps

- **Fiduciary guidance**: Advisors can serve as either a 3(21) co-fiduciary (sharing responsibility) or a 3(38) fiduciary (taking investment discretion off your plate).
- **Fee benchmarking**: Advisors compare your plan's costs to industry averages and negotiate with providers.
- **Employee education**: Advisors can run workshops, one-on-ones, and financial wellness programs.
- **Process support**: Advisors help create the IPS, organize committee meetings, and keep your Fiduciary File audit-ready.

Case Snapshot: Sloan v. Boeing Co. (2023)
What Happened?

Boeing's 401(k) plan is one of the biggest in the country, with billions in assets and hundreds of thousands of participants. A group of employees sued the company, saying the plan's investments and recordkeeping fees were too high and that the people running the plan weren't doing their jobs.

The judge didn't buy it. Why? Because Boeing could show it had a good process in place. The company:

- **Hired professional advisors** to review investments and fees,
- **Met regularly** to discuss plan performance, and
- **Documented** what they decided and why.

The court said ERISA doesn't require perfect results — just careful, well-documented decision-making. Since Boeing's team could prove they were paying attention and following a prudent process, the court dismissed most claims.

What Plan Sponsors Can Learn
- **Process beats perfection.** You don't have to guess every fund's future, but you do have to review, benchmark, and document your decisions.
- **Advisors help.** Using outside experts showed the court Boeing was serious about acting in employees' best interests.
- **Paper it up.** Keep meeting notes, reports, and fee comparisons — if it's not written down, it didn't happen.

In plain terms: Boeing won because they didn't wing it — they had professional help, a system, and solid paperwork. That's exactly what protects you, too.

Plain-Language Citation: *Sloan v. Boeing Co.*, No. 2:22-cv-00012-RSL, 2023 WL 3091995 (W.D. Wash. Apr. 26, 2023).

Action Steps for You
- Ask yourself honestly: "Do I have the expertise, time, and tools to manage this plan alone?"
- If not, interview at least three advisors who specialize in retirement plans.
- Check their fiduciary role: Are they 3(21) or 3(38)? Get it in writing.
- Make sure their compensation is transparent and reasonable.

Quick Definitions
- **3(21) Advisor:** Shares fiduciary responsibility by making recommendations, but you make the final decisions.
- **3(38) Advisor:** Has discretion to make investment decisions for the plan. You still monitor them, but they carry the liability for fund choices.
- **Fee Benchmarking:** Comparing what you pay for recordkeeping, funds, and advisory services against industry standards.

✅ **Key Takeaway:** Hiring a financial advisor isn't about giving up control — it's about gaining confidence. The right advisor keeps you compliant, makes your plan stronger, and helps your employees build real retirement security. In short, they help you avoid being the sponsor who ends up in court — or on the front page of the paper for all the wrong reasons.

Sidebar: "The Sleep-at-Night Factor"

Running a 401(k) plan alone is like driving cross-country with no GPS. You might get there, but you'll hit every pothole along the way.

A good financial advisor doesn't just manage investments — they give you peace of mind. They help you document decisions, stay compliant, educate your employees, and keep you out of hot water with the IRS or DOL.

Translation: Fewer headaches. Fewer surprises. Better outcomes for everyone.

Checklist: Is It Time to Bring in an Advisor?

- ☐ We don't have a written Investment Policy Statement (IPS).
- ☐ We haven't benchmarked plan fees in the last three years.
- ☐ Our fiduciary committee doesn't meet regularly or document decisions.
- ☐ Employees often ask financial questions we can't confidently answer.
- ☐ We've had late filings, missing forms, or other compliance hiccups.
- ☐ We don't have a structured employee education program.
- ☐ We don't know whether our current service providers are competitively priced.
- ☐ We're unsure what a 3(21) or 3(38) fiduciary even is.
- ☐ We'd like to reduce personal liability and administrative stress.
- ☐ We'd sleep better knowing a qualified fiduciary expert is watching our back.

Pro Tip:

If you checked **three or more boxes**, it's time to at least *talk* to a financial advisor. Think of it as a plan "checkup" — no different than seeing a doctor for preventive care. The goal isn't to hand over control, but to strengthen your plan and protect yourself.

APPENDIX A: CHECKLIST TO SPOT TROUBLE BEFORE THE IRS OR DOL DOES

Running a 401(k) plan means wearing a lot of hats — HR, payroll, fiduciary, and referee.

This checklist highlights the most common warning signs that get plans in trouble during audits, lawsuits, or participant complaints. If you check more than **three boxes**, it's time for a **plan compliance review**.

Plan Operations
☐ The plan document hasn't been updated or restated in the last 6 years (IRS Rev. Proc. 2021-37) or recent law changes weren't adopted on time.
☐ The plan is not being run exactly as written (eligibility, match, vesting, loans, etc.).
☐ Employee deferrals are not deposited promptly after payroll.
☐ Employer match is miscalculated or deposited late.
☐ Eligible employees are left out — or ineligible employees are included.
☐ Loans or hardship withdrawals are processed without documentation or beyond plan limits.
☐ HR or payroll can't explain the plan's definition of compensation.
☐ Form 5500 was filed late or not filed at all.

Fiduciary Oversight
☐ There is no formal fiduciary committee or no written meeting minutes.
☐ There is no written Investment Policy Statement (IPS) to guide fund decisions.
☐ Fees haven't been reviewed or benchmarked in the past few years.
☐ The investment lineup hasn't been reviewed or updated recently.
☐ Fiduciary training hasn't been provided or documented.
☐ Service-provider contracts haven't been reviewed or renewed in several years.

☐ There is no fiduciary liability insurance policy in place.
☐ The roles of fiduciaries (plan sponsor, trustee, 3(21), or 3(38) advisor) are unclear.

Administrative & Legal Compliance
☐ Fidelity bond is missing or too small (must cover at least 10 % of plan assets handled, minimum $1,000, maximum $500,000 — $1 million if the plan holds employer stock).
☐ Employee census and payroll data aren't reconciled each year.
☐ The plan has 100 + eligible participants but no annual audit (unless the 80–120 rule applies).
☐ Required participant notices (safe harbor, QDIA, 404a-5 fee notice) aren't sent on time.
☐ Nondiscrimination tests (ADP/ACP or top-heavy) consistently fail or lack documentation.
☐ Service-provider fees haven't been reviewed for reasonableness.

Governance & Cybersecurity
☐ Vendor SOC 1 / SSAE-18 reports are not reviewed each year.
☐ There is no written cybersecurity or data-protection procedure.
☐ Service providers (recordkeeper, TPA) haven't been vetted for security and compliance.
☐ The plan has no process for finding "missing participants" or returning unclaimed accounts.

Participant Experience
☐ Fewer than **75 % of eligible employees** are participating.
☐ Average employee savings rate is **below 5 %**.
☐ Employees complain about confusing investments or high fees.
☐ No financial-education or wellness program is offered.

If You Checked Three or More Boxes
Your plan could face audit findings, penalties, or fiduciary exposure. Schedule a 401(k) Compliance Review with your plan advisor or third-party administrator to document fixes and strengthen your fiduciary process.

Pro Tip: Keep a Fiduciary File with your plan document, amendments, fee reviews, IPS, testing results, 5500 filings, and meeting minutes. If the DOL shows up, a well-organized file is your best defense.

Compliance Note: This checklist is intended for internal plan administration and fiduciary oversight. It is not legal, tax, or investment advice. Review findings with your plan advisor, third-party administrator, or ERISA attorney before making plan changes.

ABOUT THE AUTHOR

Craig C. Brigman, EA, AIF®, CEPA®
is a Wealth Advisor and Partner specializing in 401(k) fiduciary
strategy, plan design, and compliance. With over two decades
helping business owners and HR leaders solve problems and build
better retirement plans, Craig blends tax strategy, practical
guidance, and plain talk to make complex rules simple — and
compliance achievable.

Craig C. Brigman, EA, AIF®, CEPA®, CDFA®
(540) 581 – 8273
6701 Peters Creek Rd, Suite 107, Roanoke, VA 24019
craig.brigman@dw-advisors.com
www.destinationwealthadvisors.com

Made in the USA
Middletown, DE
03 March 2026